Book Nook News

by Derek Scott
illustrated by Meredith Thomas

Harcourt
SCHOOL PUBLISHERS

Printed in Mexico

ISBN 10: 0-15-351413-2
ISBN 13: 978-0-15-351413-5

Ordering Options
ISBN 10: 0-15-351212-1 (Grade 2 Advanced Collection)
ISBN 13: 978-0-15-351212-4 (Grade 2 Advanced Collection)
ISBN 10: 0-15-358048-8 (package of 5)
ISBN 13: 978-0-15-358048-2 (package of 5)

2 3 4 5 6 7 8 9 10 050 15 14 13 12 11 10 09 08 07

Characters

Mr. Jackson

Mrs. Coats

Mr. Reed

Anchor 1

Anchor 2

Red Riding Hood

Wolf

Setting: On the school stage

Mr. Jackson: Is everyone ready to present our news? Action!

Anchor 1: Good morning, and welcome to *Book Week News*.

Anchor 2: This news report is brought to you by the children of room eight, Lakeside School.

Anchor 1: Today we will talk to some people about Book Week.

Anchor 2: We have Mrs. Coats, our librarian, in the studio right now. Welcome to *Book Week News*, Mrs. Coats. What's happening in the library this week?

Mrs. Coats: We have over one hundred new books on display for Book Week.

Anchor 1: Can the children take the new books home, Mrs. Coats?

Mrs. Coats: This week is for looking at the books. Beginning next week, the children will be able to take them home.

Anchor 2: I believe that you have another interesting activity in the library.

Mrs. Coats: Oh, yes. Every day at lunch, we have a storyteller coming to the library. I think she will prove to be very entertaining for all.

Anchor 1: Thank you, Mrs. Coats. I'm sure everyone will like the storyteller and the new books.

Anchor 2: Now we would like to interview Mr. Reed, principal of Lakeside School. Good morning, Mr. Reed. I guess you're excited about this special week.

Mr. Reed: Good morning. I'm *very* excited about Book Week. All the children have been so creative in getting ready for it. The older children have been learning about authors, and they have been making colorful book jackets and bookmarks. The younger children have been making picture books.

Anchor 1: Mr. Reed, are we going to be able to go through the classrooms to look at everything?

Mr. Reed: Yes, everyone is welcome to visit the classrooms.

Anchor 2: Gosh! Look who's here!

Sometimes we *do* get surprise guests!

Anchor 1: Are you two here for Book Week?

Red Riding Hood: Yes, and we are already in costume for the book character parade on Friday.

Wolf: I'll be leading the parade! I hope that everyone will dress up as his or her favorite book character and follow me around the school.

Anchor 1: I hope that it will be safe for the students to follow you, Wolf!

Anchor 2: The parade certainly sounds entertaining! We all wish Lakeside School a successful Book Week.

Anchor 1: This is *Book Week News* from Lakeside School.

Mr. Jackson: Great work, team!

Think Critically

1. What tells you that this story is a Readers' Theater?
2. Who was presenting the news and why?
3. Which adults did the children talk to about Book Week?
4. When was the Book Parade going to be?
5. Which character from a book would you dress up as in a parade? Why?

Social Studies

Write Questions Think of a book that you like. Write three questions you would like to ask the author of this book.

School-Home Connection Tell a family member about the story. Then talk about special events that take place at your school.

Word Count: 418